Published by Christian Focus Publications Ltd
Geanies House, Fearn, Tain, Ross-shire IV20 1TW www.christianfocus.com

Copyright © John Brown Brian Wright
ISBN: 978-1-5271-0945-2

This edition published in 2023
Cover illustration and internal illustrations by Lisa Flanagan
Cover and internal design by Lisa Flanagan
Printed and bound in China

JONAH'S
journeys

John Brown
Brian Wright

And it happened long ago that
a man named Jonah
lived near Nazareth,
where Jesus grew up.

One day God told Jonah,
"Get up! **Go to Nineveh**,
the great city, and warn them that
I know how bad they've been."

So Jonah got up and went ...
but **not to Nineveh!**
Instead, he went in the opposite
direction. God said to go northeast to
Nineveh, but Jonah boarded a ship
sailing southwest to Tarshish.

◁ TARSHISH

So God sent a great storm
that was tearing the ship apart!

Then the crew cast lots to find out
who was to blame for the storm,
and **it was Jonah's fault!**"

The sailors tried to row back to shore,
but **the storm was too strong**.

So they prayed, "**O Lord, please don't punish us because of him!**"

Then they picked Jonah up and threw him into the sea.
As soon as they did,
the storm stopped!
And they offered a sacrifice and made vows to Jonah's God.

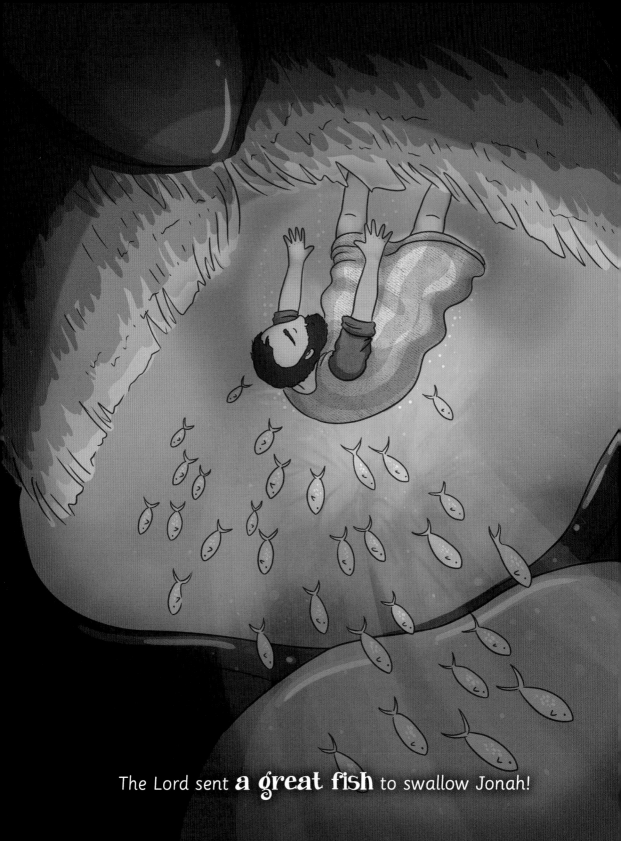

The Lord sent **a great fish** to swallow Jonah!

And Jonah spent
three days and nights
in the fish's stomach.

Then, when Jonah could sink no lower, he prayed:

"When I was in trouble, I cried out to God,
and He answered me!

I called to you from the deep,
and You heard me!"

"You threw me into the deep
and buried me beneath your waves.
But even though you cast me from You,
still I will look to you for rescue!"

"Water covered me;
seaweed wrapped around my head.
I sank down to the bottom of the sea
and was trapped."

"But **you brought me back**,
O Lord my God,
even from this deep pit!
While I was slipping away,
I remembered the Lord,
and you heard my prayer!"

"Those who worship false gods
miss out on the mercy they could have had.
But as for me,
I will offer a sacrifice of thanksgiving,
for **salvation belongs to the Lord!**"

As soon as Jonah finished praying, the Lord
commanded the fish to spit Jonah out onto dry land.

God again told Jonah, "Get up! Go to Nineveh, the
great city, and say to them what I tell you."
And **this time Jonah obeyed** and went.

Jonah went into the massive city of Nineveh
and shouted out God's message:

The people of **Nineveh believed God and repented**. They stopped eating food and put on black, scratchy clothing to show they were sad for being so bad.

Even the king repented! He took off his robe and put on a black, scratchy shirt and sat in ashes. Then he issued an order for the entire city:

"Let no one eat a bite or drink a drop, not even animals!

Everyone must wear scratchy clothes, even our animals.

Everyone stop doing bad things and hurting people and ask God to spare us!"

"Who knows? When God sees how sorry we are for being bad, **maybe He will stop being angry** at us and decide not to destroy us."

When God saw the Ninevites repent, **He was merciful** and did not destroy them.

Jonah was angry, however, and left the city to see
what would happen. "I knew you would show mercy, Lord!
That's why I ran away! I'd rather die than live!"

The Lord **God sent a plant** to shade Jonah from the sun. Jonah was happy about the plant.

The next day, though, **God sent a worm** to eat the plant. Then **God sent a scorching wind**, and as the sun beat down Jonah grew faint and said, "I'd rather die than live!"

Then God said to Jonah,
"Are you right to be angry that the plant died?"

You care about this plant, which you didn't cause to grow
and which lived and died in a day.

Should I not care about Nineveh, which has more than 120,000 people who do not know right from wrong, plus all the animals?"

God taught Jonah some **important lessons**, which we need to learn as well. We should **care for all people**, because God cares for all people — even those who do bad things, like the Ninevites.

We should **never run away from God!**
We should obey Him instantly, completely, and cheerfully,
no matter what He tells us to do.

We should **pray to God** no matter what we've done or
what situation we're in. The Lord is sovereign over storms and
seas, fish and plants, winds and worms — over everything!
And He is gracious to forgive us when we repent of our sins.

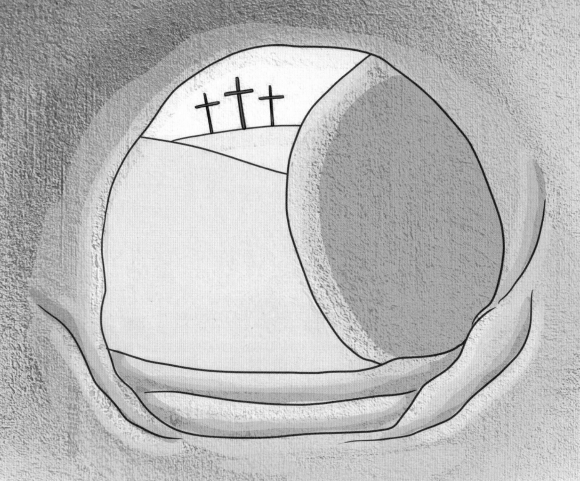

This is why God sent His Son Jesus, who died on the cross for our sins and then rose from the dead. And do you know what Jesus called His resurrection? **"The sign of Jonah".**

Just as Jonah spent three days in the great fish, so Jesus spent three days in the grave.

But Jonah only seemed to come back from the dead, whereas Jesus actually died and rose again! Jesus was indeed **"something greater than Jonah"!**

So when you think of Jonah, think of Jesus.
And remember that God who loved the
Ninevites so much that He sent Jonah to
warn them, loves you so much that
He sent Jesus to save you.

Jonah was right —
Salvation is from the Lord!

Christian Focus Publications publishes books for adults and children under its four main imprints: Christian Focus, CF4K, Mentor, and Christian Heritage. Our books reflect our conviction that God's Word is reliable and that Jesus is the way to know Him, and live for ever with Him.

Our children's publication list covers pre-school to early teens. We also publish personal and family devotionals, biographies and inspirational stories that children will love.

From pre-school board books to teenage apologetics, we have it covered!

Christian Focus Publications Ltd,
Geanies House, Fearn, Ross-shire,
IV20 1TW, Scotland,
United Kingdom.
www.christianfocus.com

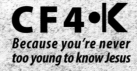

CF4•K
*Because you're never
too young to know Jesus*